The Serpent and the Saint

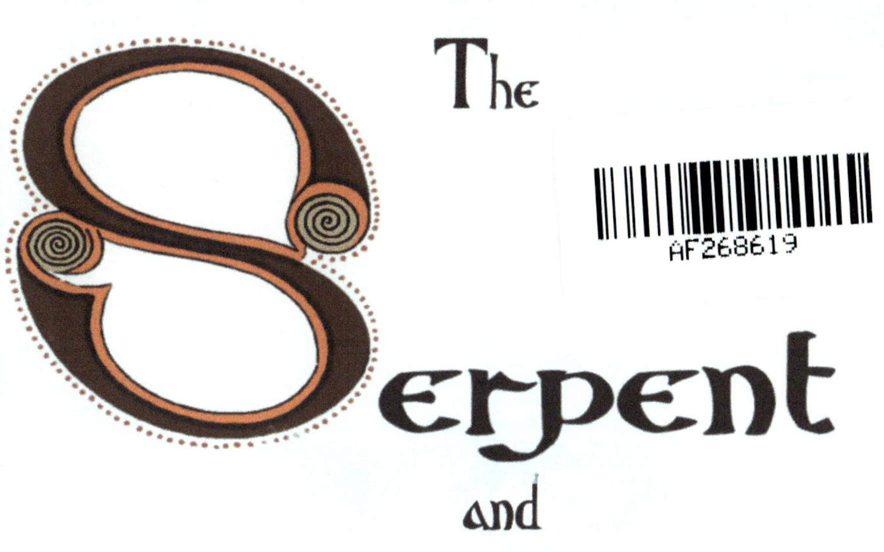

Written By C.L. Redding

Illustrated by Olivia Wylie

ISBN 978-1-7343271-4-4
Written by C.L. Redding
Illustrated by Olivia Wylie
Copyright 2021 Christine Redding

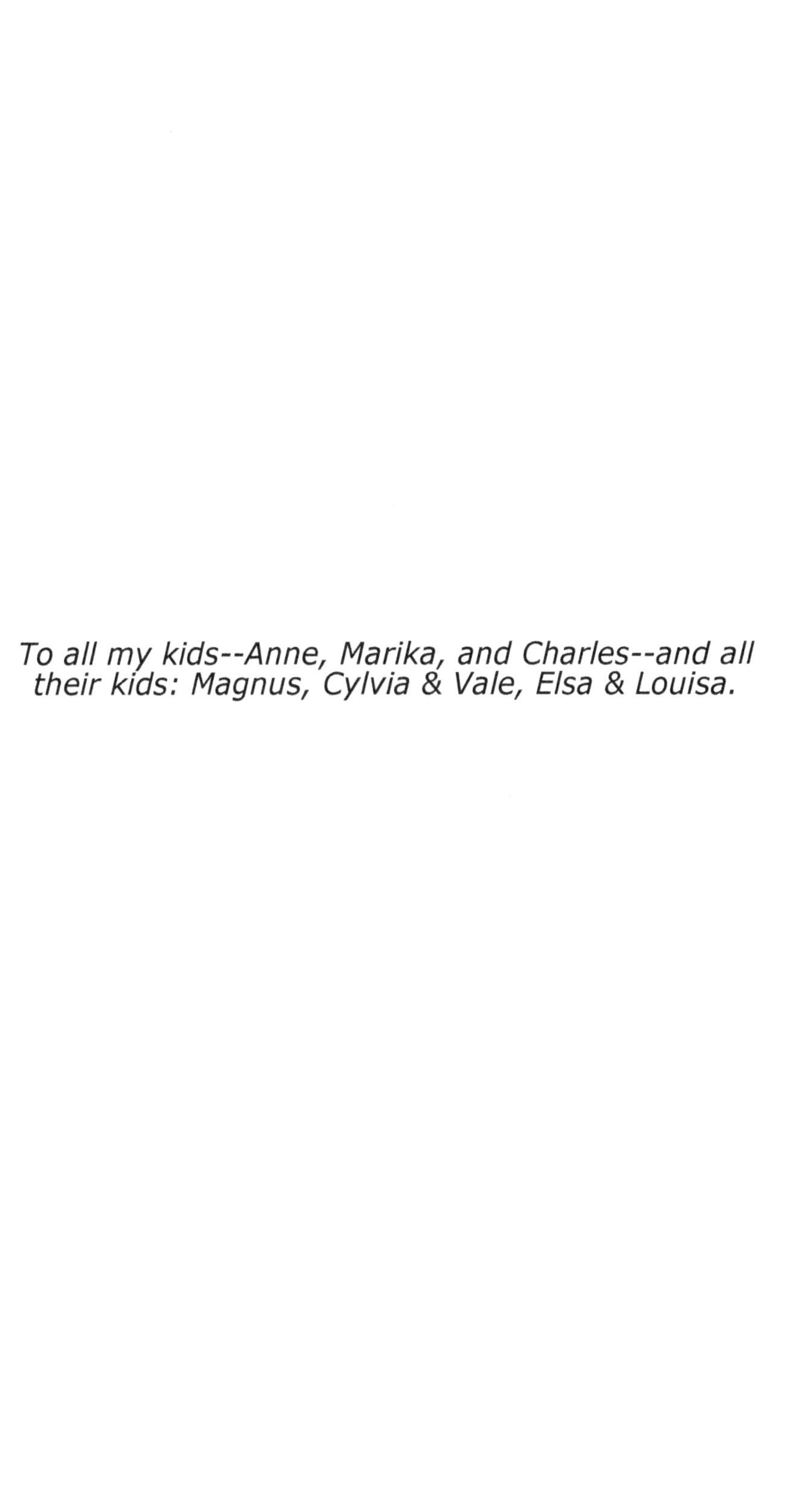

To all my kids--Anne, Marika, and Charles--and all their kids: Magnus, Cylvia & Vale, Elsa & Louisa.

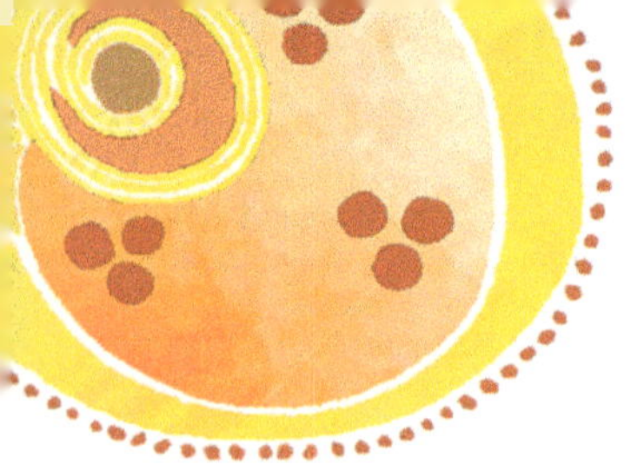

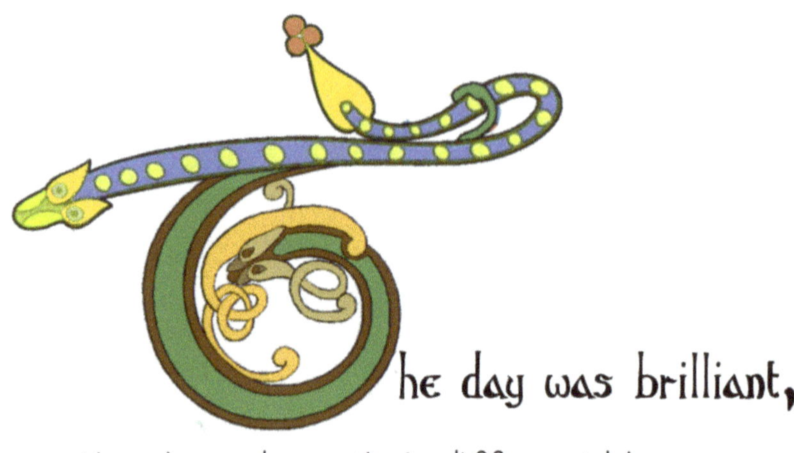

The day was brilliant,
the sky and sea their different blues,
the lands bright green under the sun and rich
brown where crops would soon be growing.

But the Saint, sitting high on the tor above
the landscape, saw nothing of the loveliness
There was a morose look upon him.
Beside him was his tall shepherd's crook,
and a great tome bound in dark leather
sat unopened upon his lap.

The rich scents of early spring
wafted on the breeze.

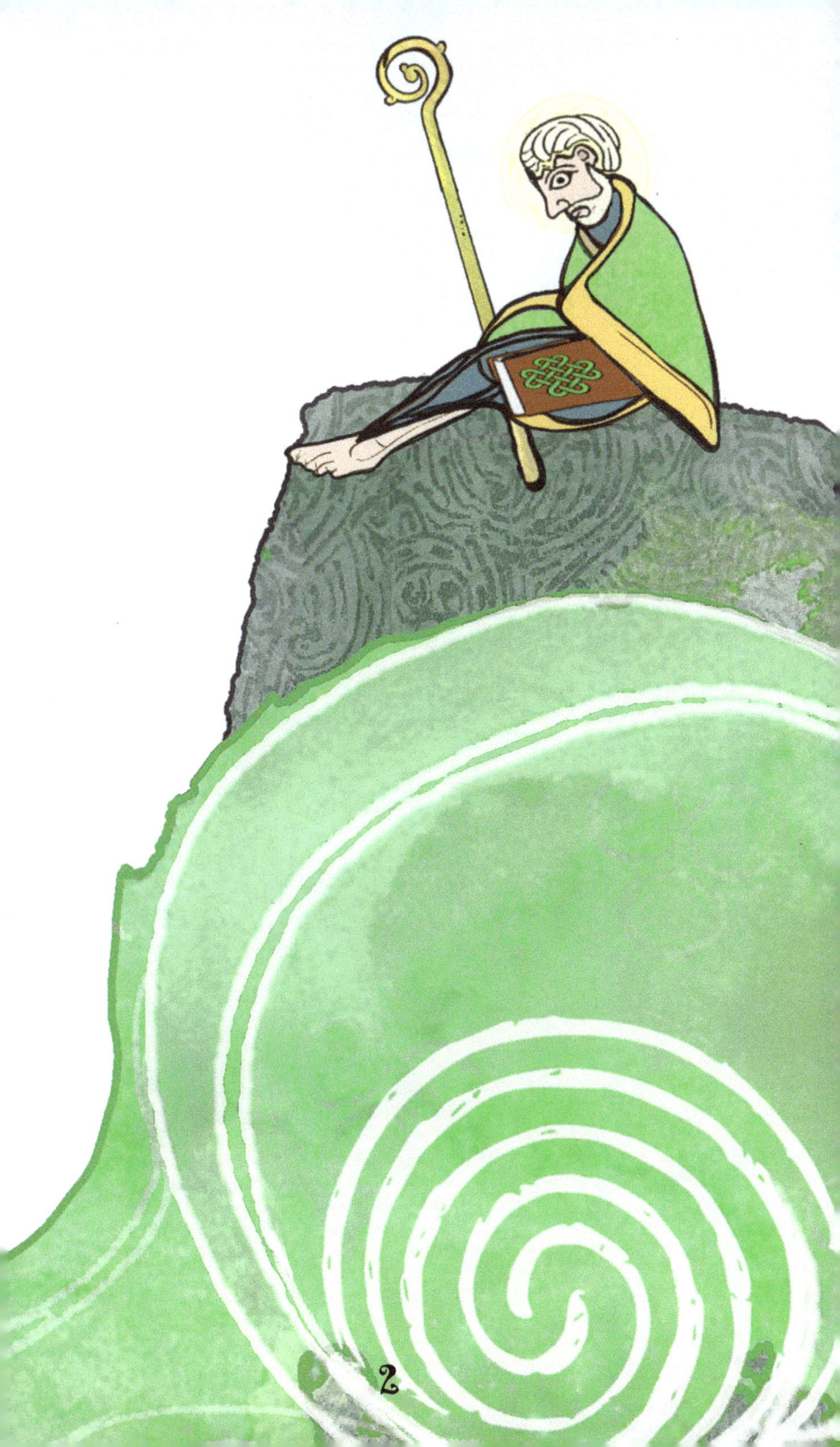

As he sat there upon the jutting
stone, a smooth motion caught his eye. A
great serpent slid up onto the same rocky
perch.Sunlight glinted off its patterned back,
its colors all of gold and ruby,
flecks of sapphire here and
emerald there.

The serpent offered no harm,
but settled in the sunlight to bask.
In the warmth,
it seemed to sigh.

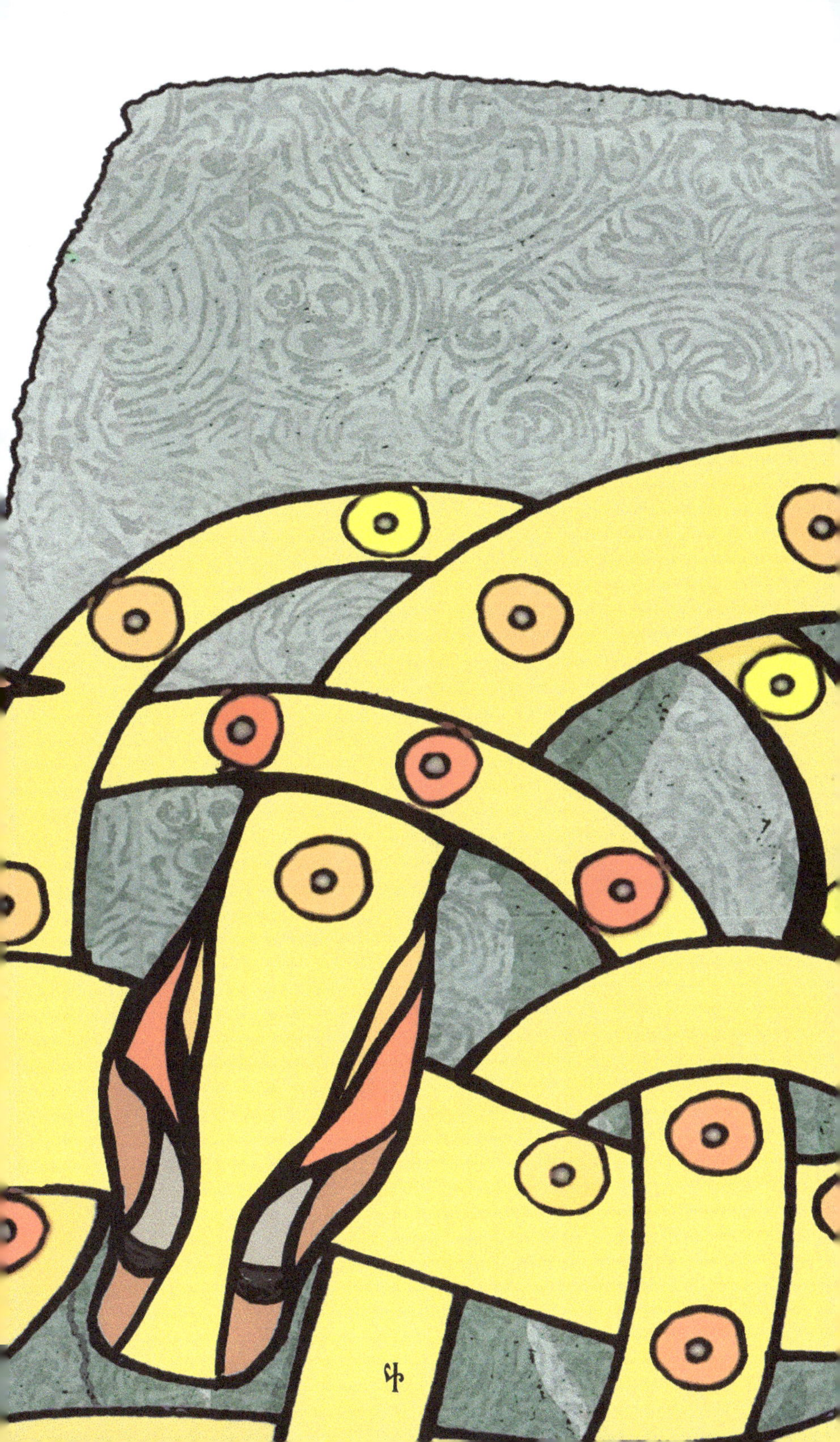

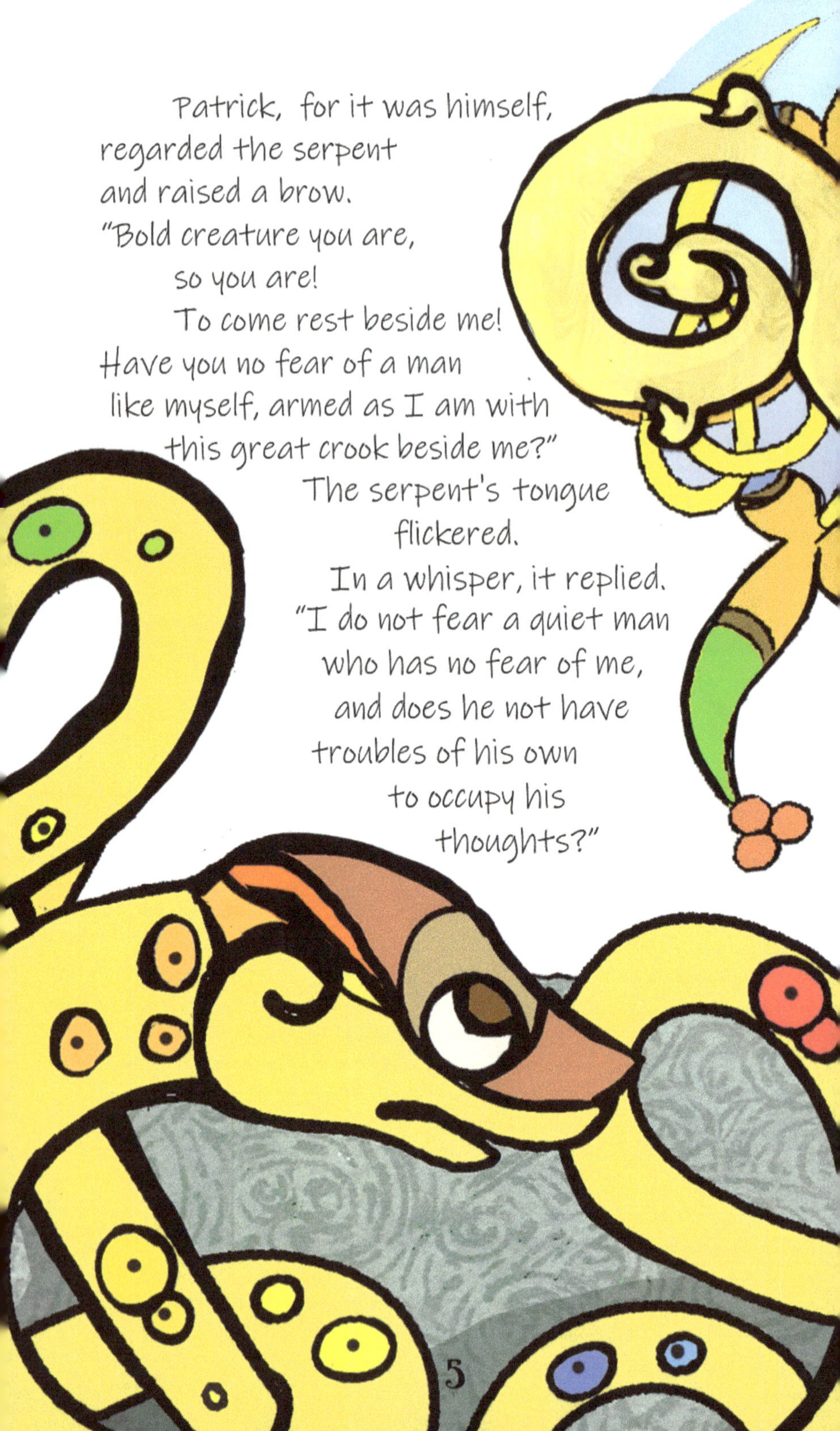

Patrick, for it was himself,
regarded the serpent
and raised a brow.
"Bold creature you are,
so you are!
To come rest beside me!
Have you no fear of a man
like myself, armed as I am with
this great crook beside me?"
The serpent's tongue
flickered.
In a whisper, it replied.
"I do not fear a quiet man
who has no fear of me,
and does he not have
troubles of his own
to occupy his
thoughts?"

5

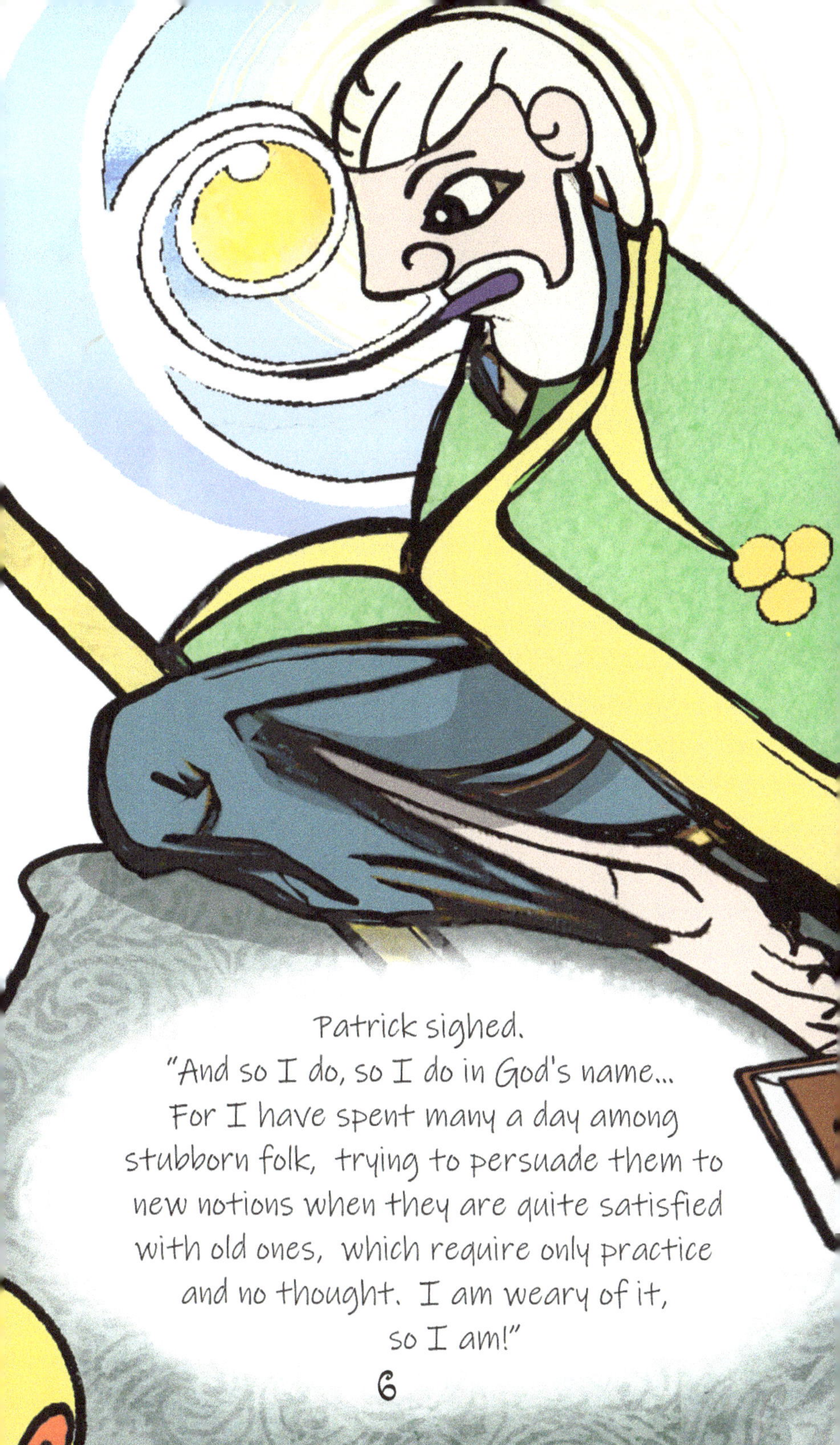

Patrick sighed.
"And so I do, so I do in God's name...
For I have spent many a day among
stubborn folk, trying to persuade them to
new notions when they are quite satisfied
with old ones, which require only practice
and no thought. I am weary of it,
so I am!"

6

He looked again at the serpent, and with narrowing eyes. "And don't you be trying me with your blandishments and wiles, for it is never giving up my mission that I intend, no matter the obstinacy of these wild folk!"
The serpent raised its head.
"It's no purpose of mine to trouble your path, Man. Don't I have my own troubles upon me, after all?

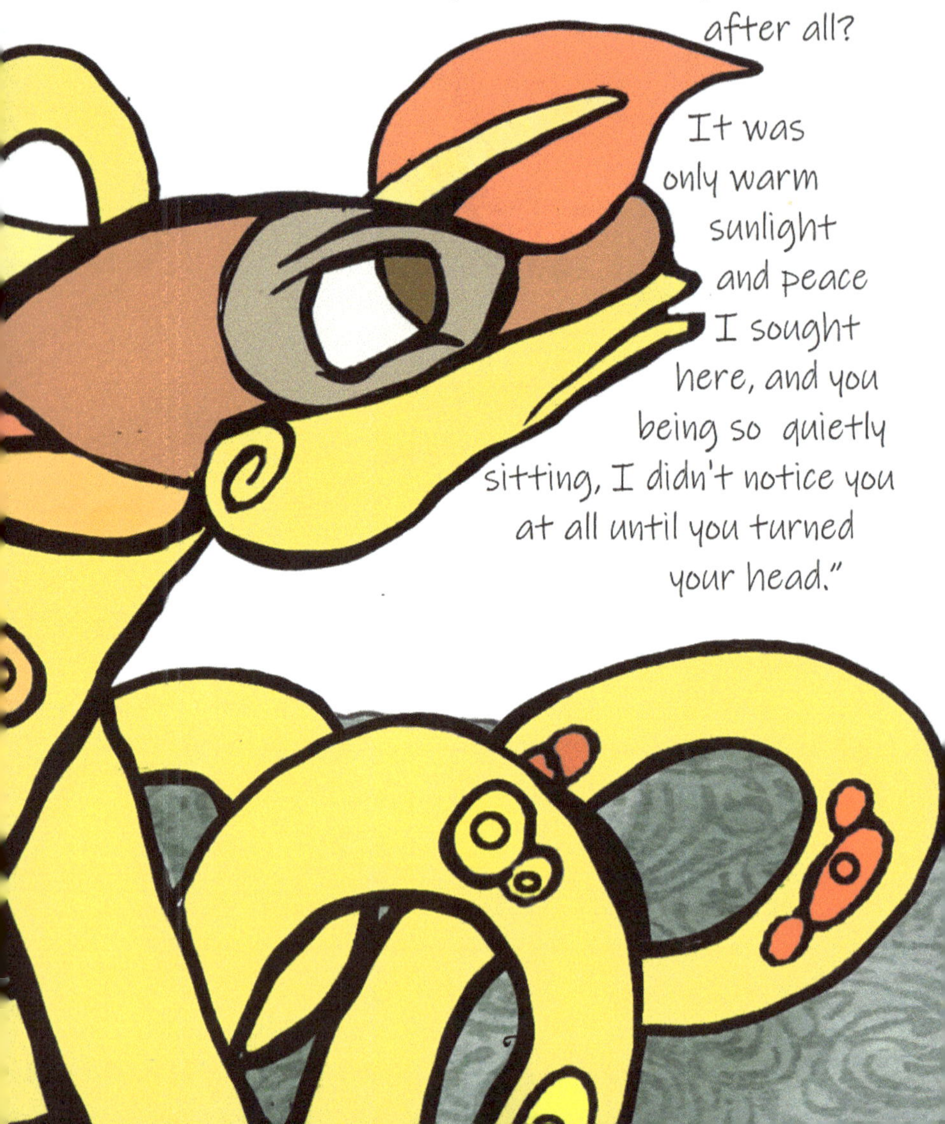

It was only warm sunlight and peace I sought here, and you being so quietly sitting, I didn't notice you at all until you turned your head."

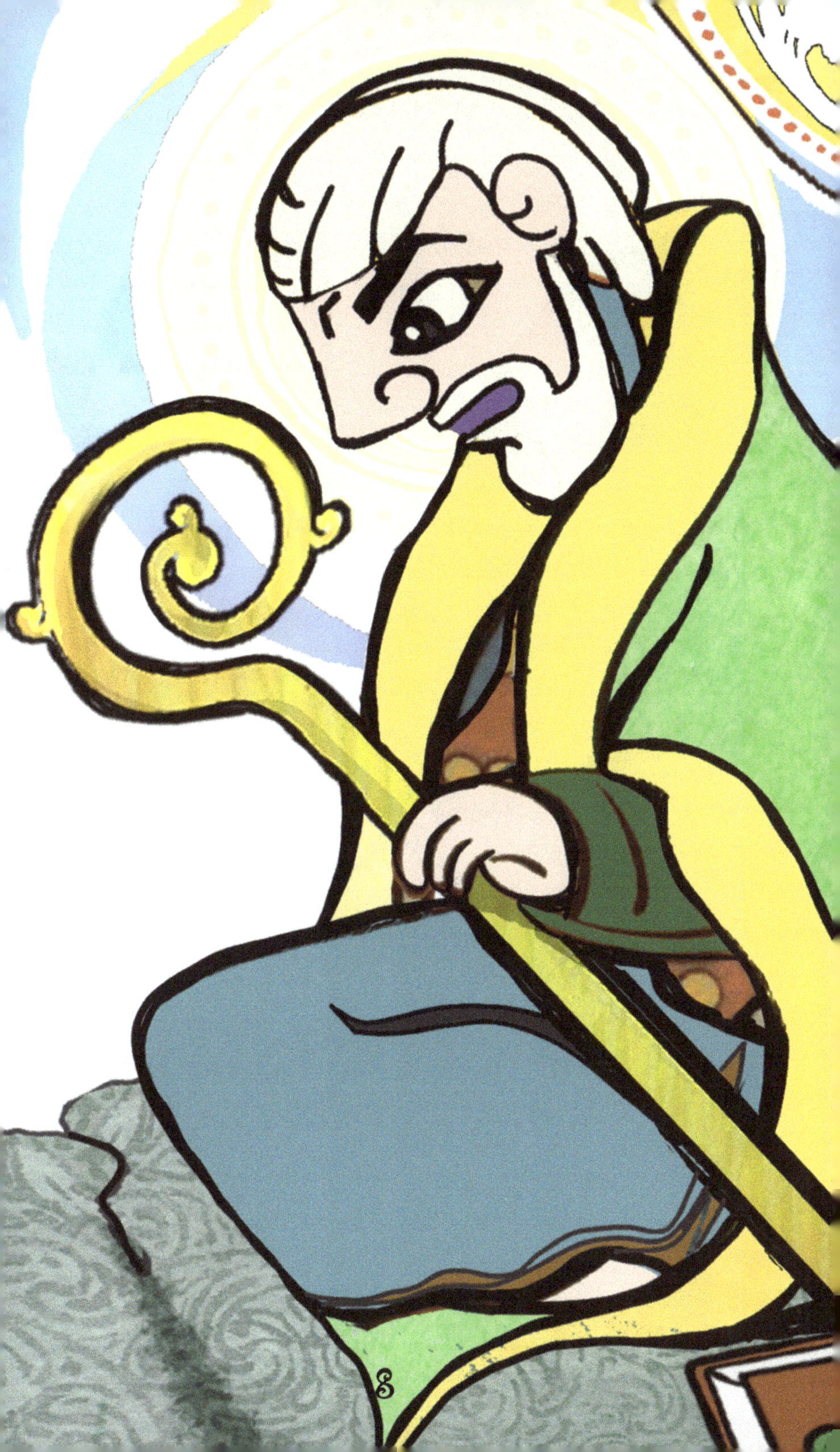

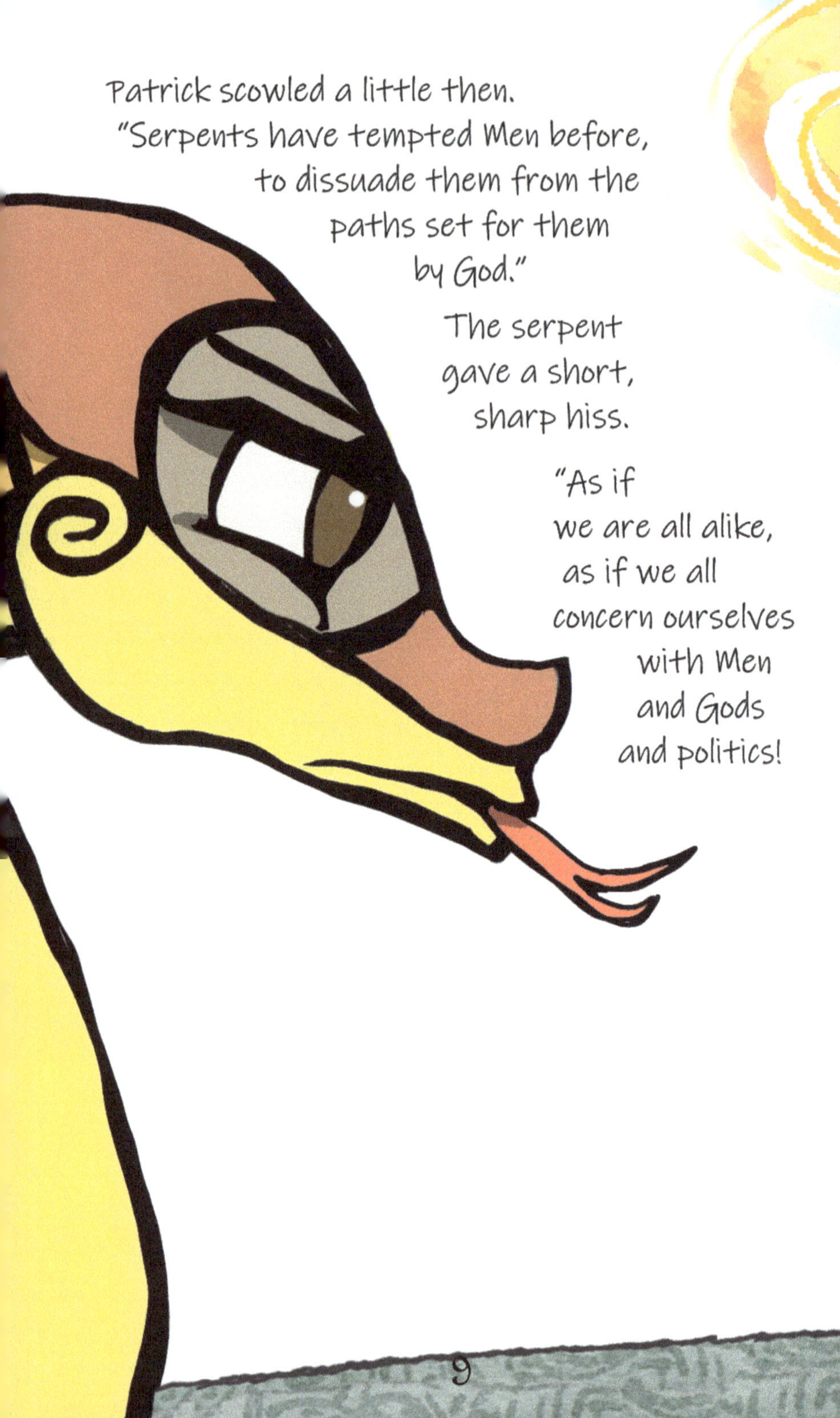

Patrick scowled a little then. "Serpents have tempted Men before, to dissuade them from the paths set for them by God."

The serpent gave a short, sharp hiss.

"As if we are all alike, as if we all concern ourselves with Men and Gods and politics!

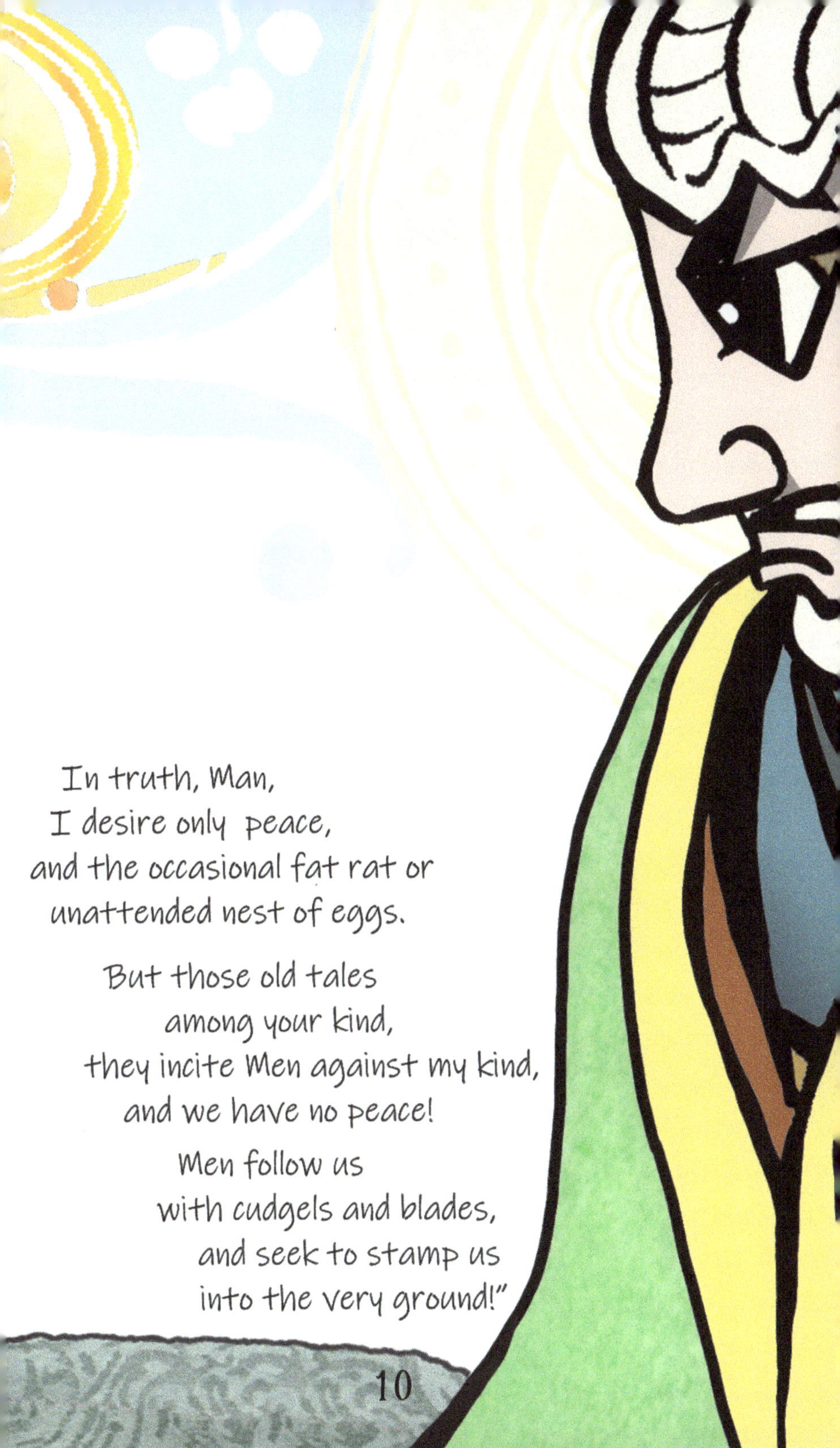

In truth, Man,
I desire only peace,
and the occasional fat rat or
unattended nest of eggs.

But those old tales
among your kind,
they incite Men against my kind,
and we have no peace!

Men follow us
with cudgels and blades,
and seek to stamp us
into the very ground!"

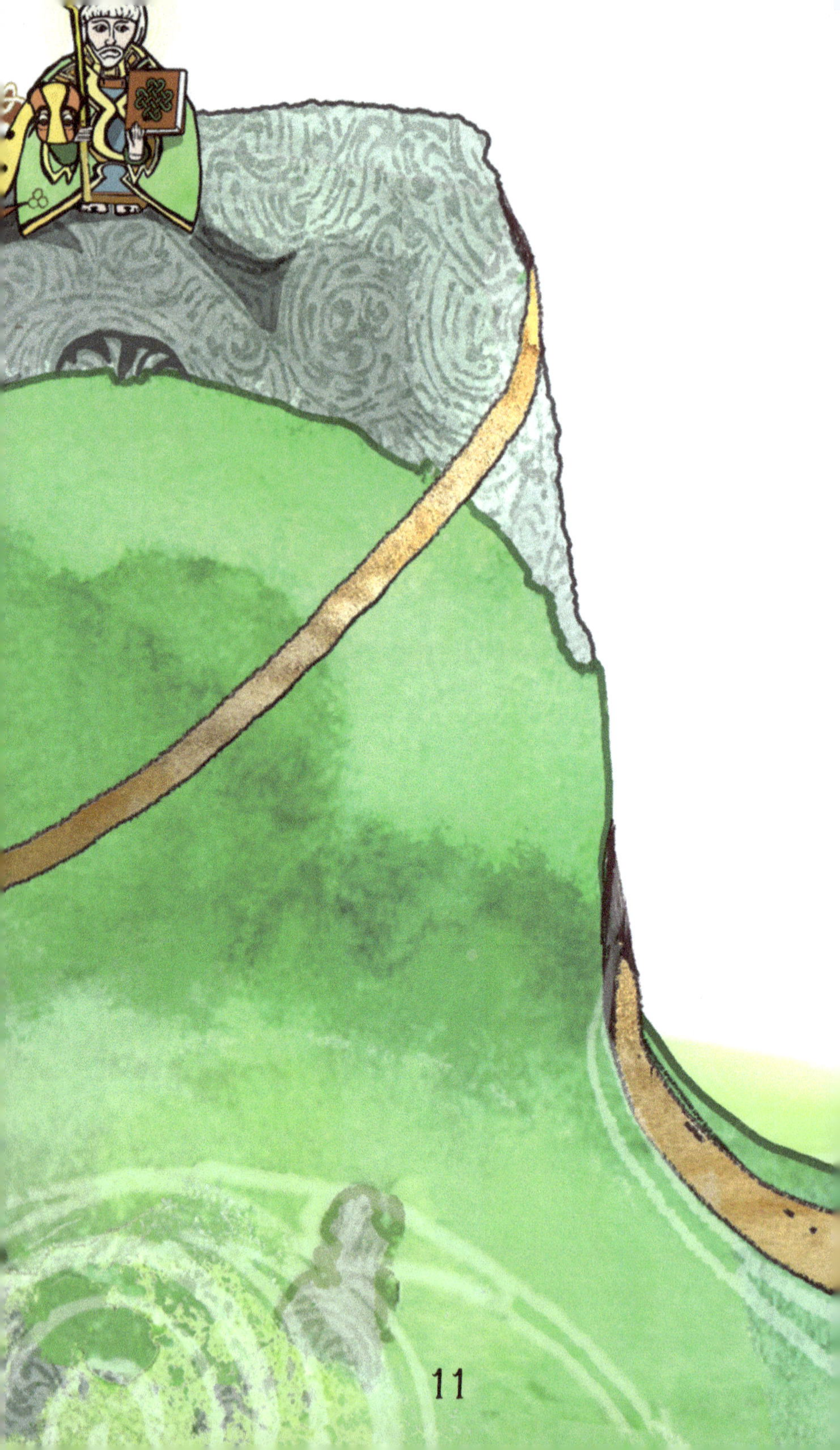

It raised its head and pointed,
        "See you there, men coming
                along the road...?"

        And it was so:
a handful of men came bearing farming tools,
fierce as they followed the road that wound
            around the tor, up to where
        the Saint and the serpent sat
        in the sun.
        "Someone saw me, so they did, as I passed
        through the fields," the Serpent said,
            "and now they go out of their way to
                    destroy my peace
                        and myself."

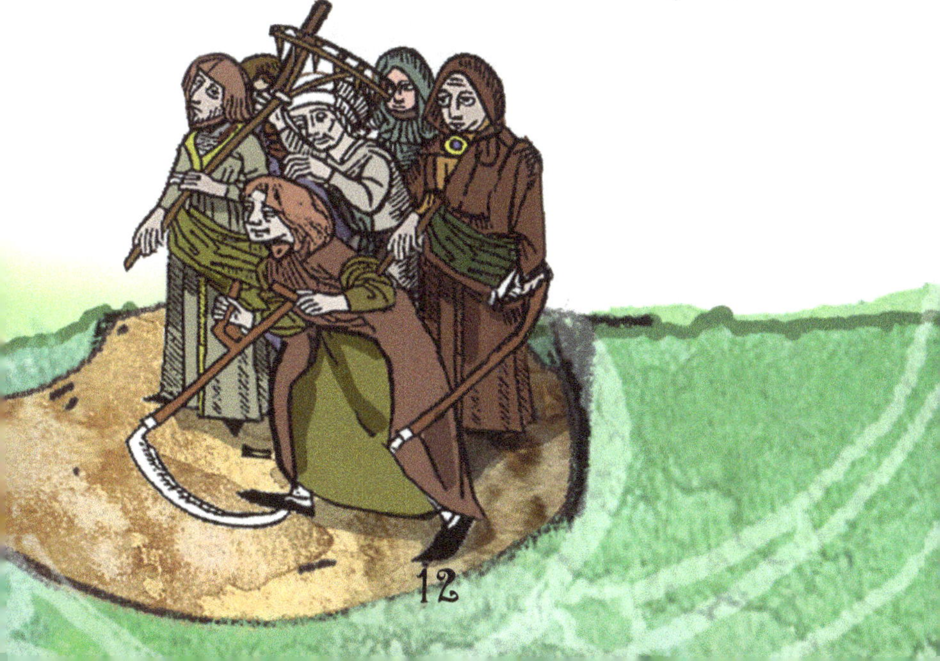

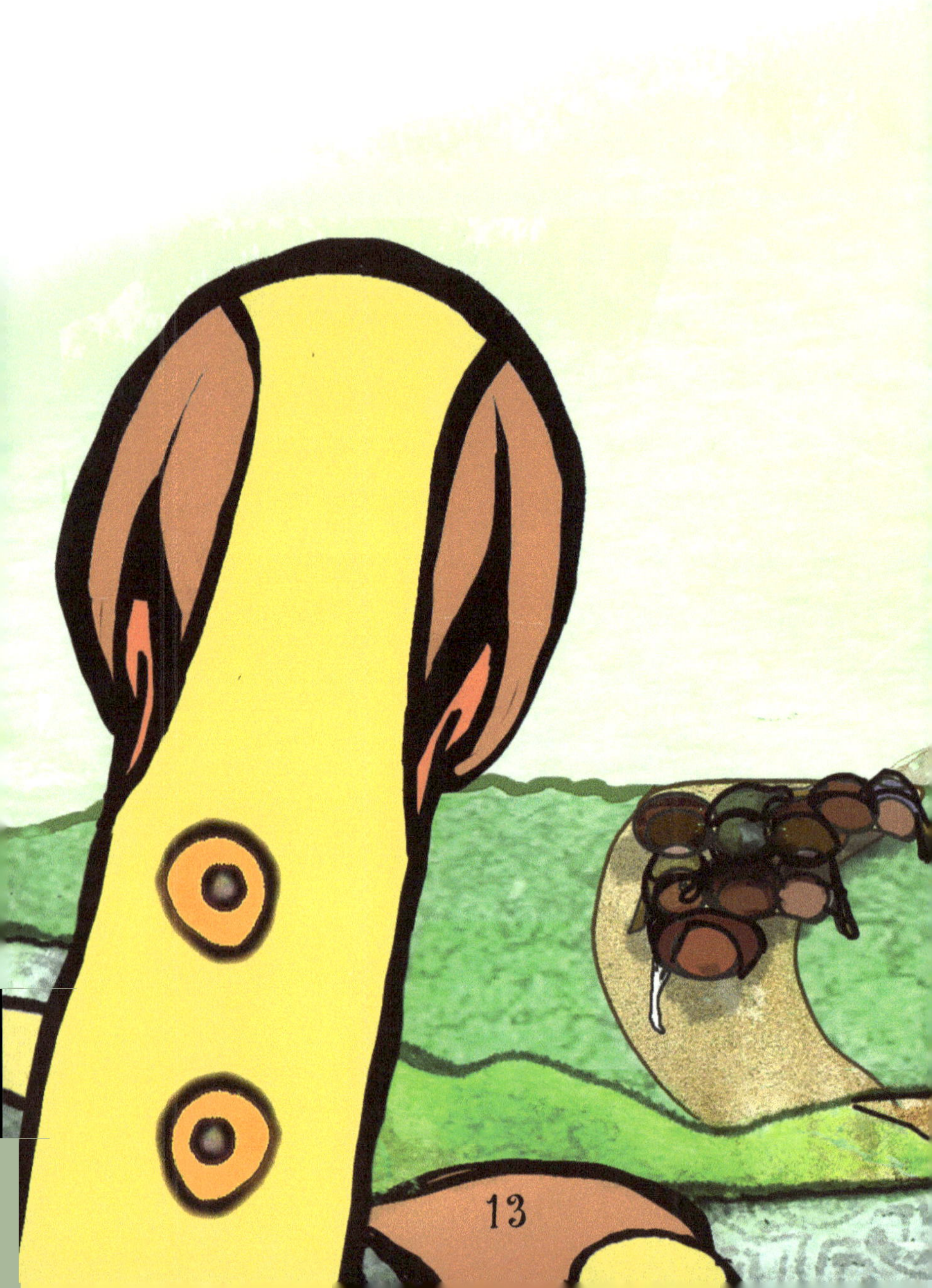

Patrick looked at the men, and at the serpent.
"You might flee faster than they come,
and hide yourself within these rocks."

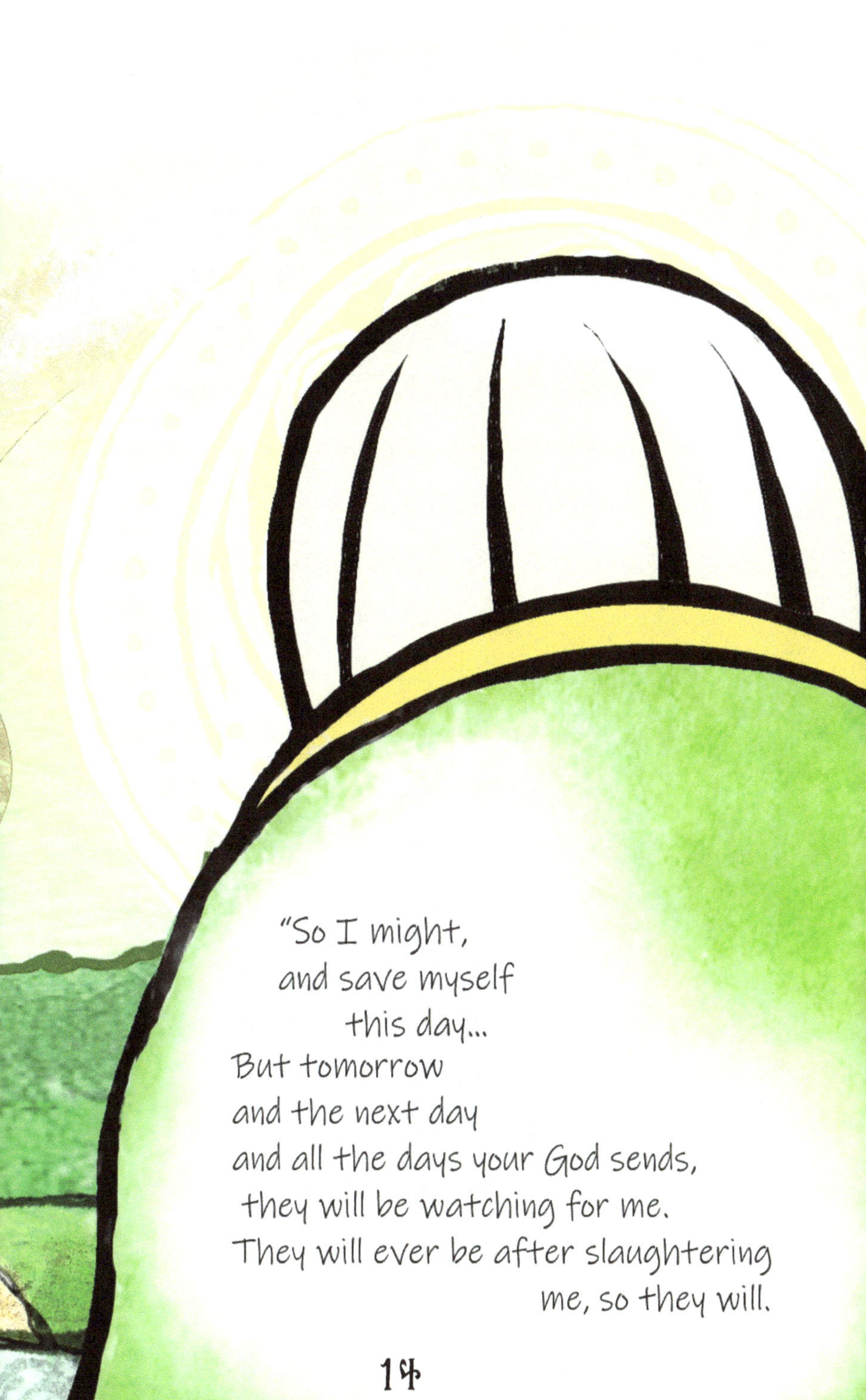
"So I might,
and save myself
this day...
But tomorrow
and the next day
and all the days your God sends,
they will be watching for me.
They will ever be after slaughtering
me, so they will.

19

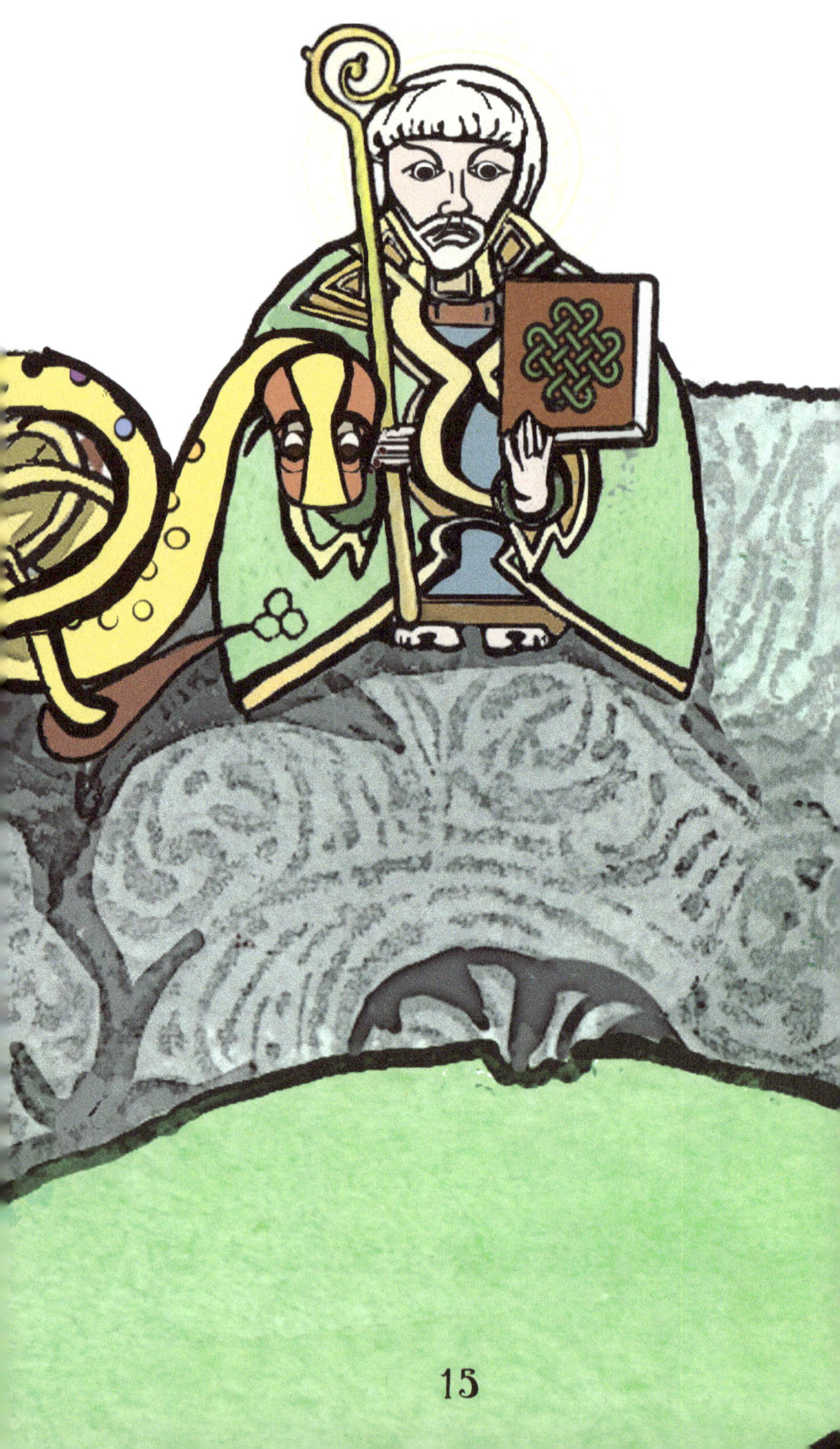

The Saint scowled again.
"So they are, the obstinate things! I would not
have them slay you, Serpent, for you are old
and I am thinking you are wise, too, in your
way. And peace is a worthy goal where there is
nothing just to fight for.

I would not stop you fighting for your
life, but they are many, and from here
I can see they have no mercy in them.
They are simple folk, too busy
at their own lives to care for your
beauty and value it.
And sure, they do believe those old
tales of evil and ill-doings, as if
they are not merely parables."

The crowd below were closer,
rising up onto the knees of
the tor, and soon would be
at its shoulders.
They raised voices of anger
and intentions of no good
towards the Saint's
companion.

The serpent sighed "Sorry I am,
Man, that I must take my leave, for I
have enjoyed your company and our brief
speech together."

"And will you run then? Slither
away again today, and tomorrow, and
all the days God sends?"

The serpent shuddered along its length:
a snake's way of shrugging, for it is
all shoulder, after all.

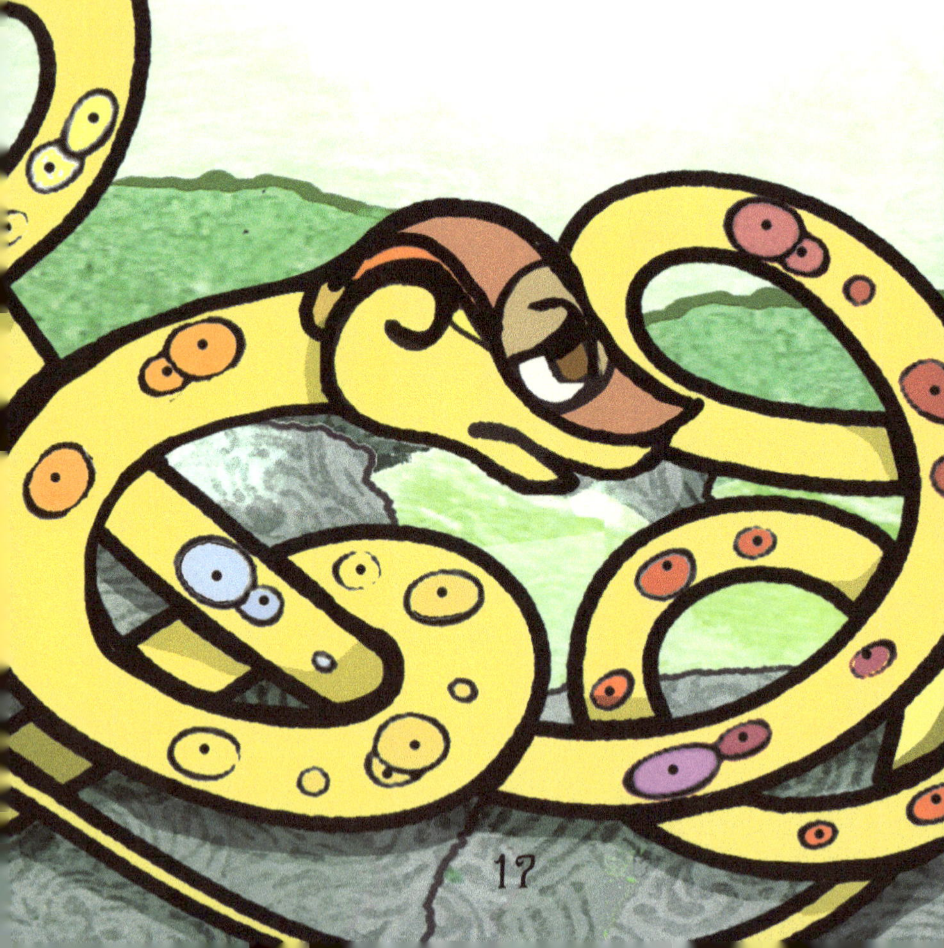

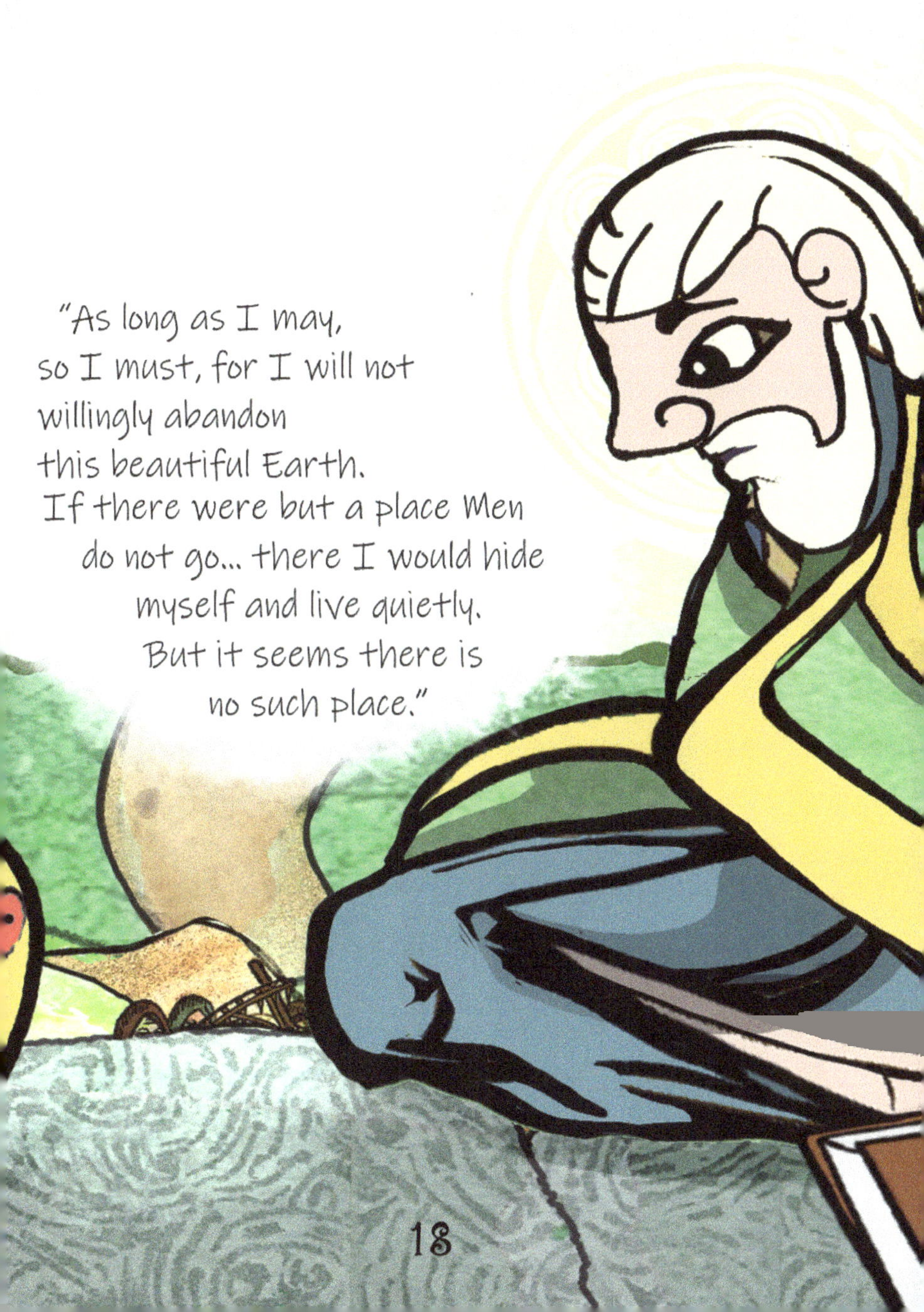
"As long as I may,
so I must, for I will not
willingly abandon
this beautiful Earth.
If there were but a place Men
do not go... there I would hide
myself and live quietly.
But it seems there is
no such place."

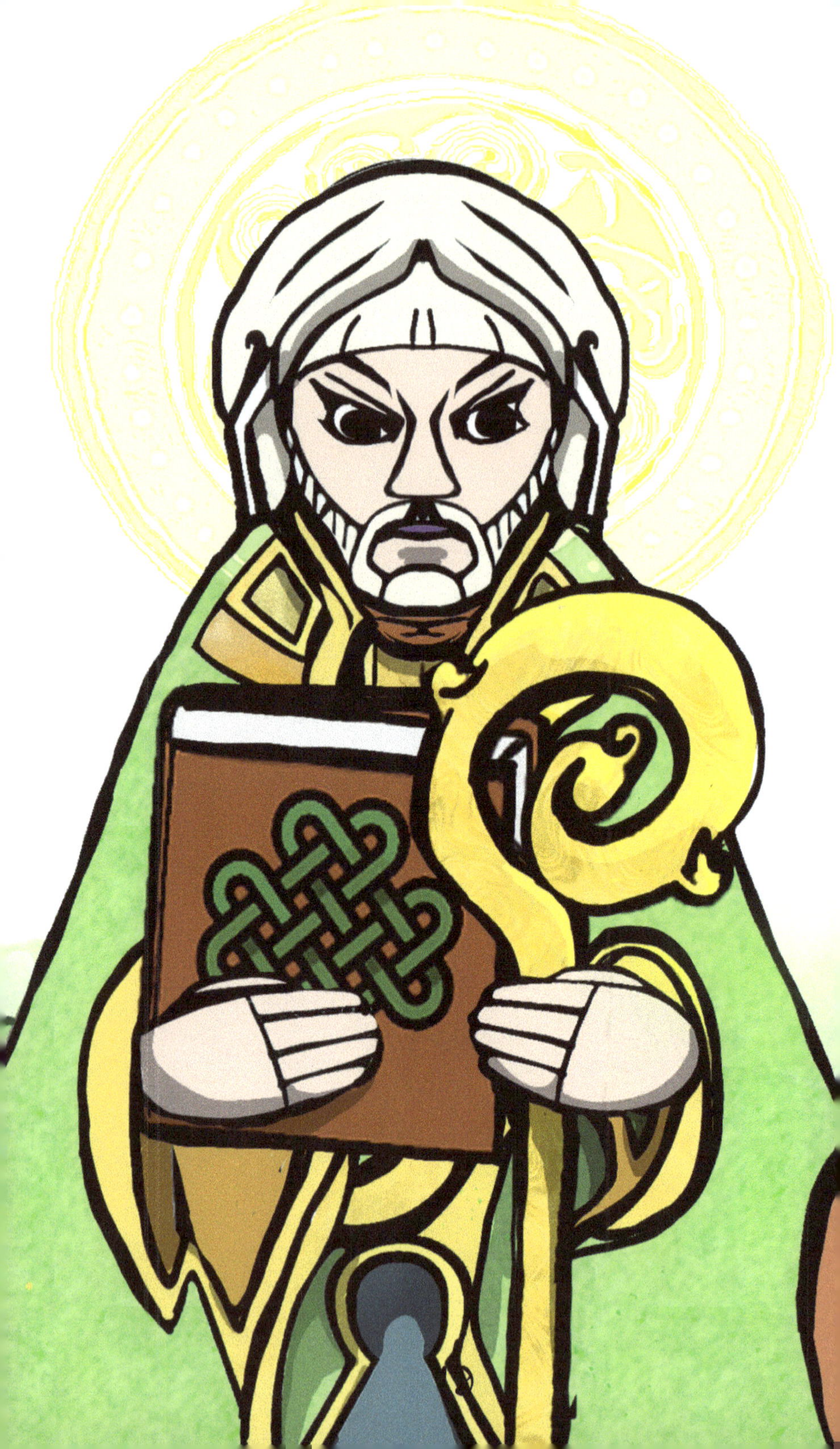

Then Patrick, all ascowl, lifted an
eyebrow and put a hand upon the
great book beside him.

"I know a place they will not go,
no matter how I plead and promise,
threaten and cajole...
It's a new and wondrous truth
I'm after giving them, though they
see it only through the eyes of fear."
The voices were louder now, though the
men could not be seen, for the road led
back around the tor as it rose.

In a moment they would come over the
top and spy their quarry there,
beside the Saint.

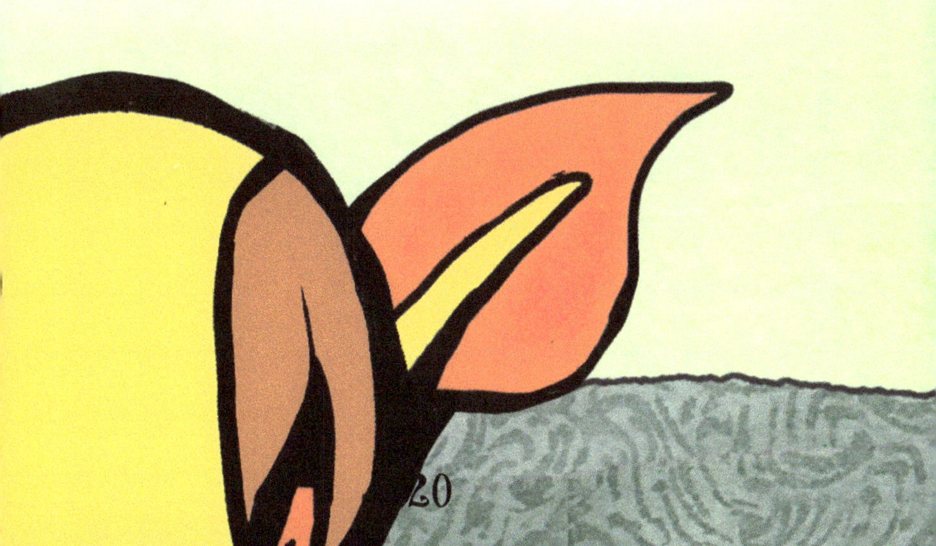

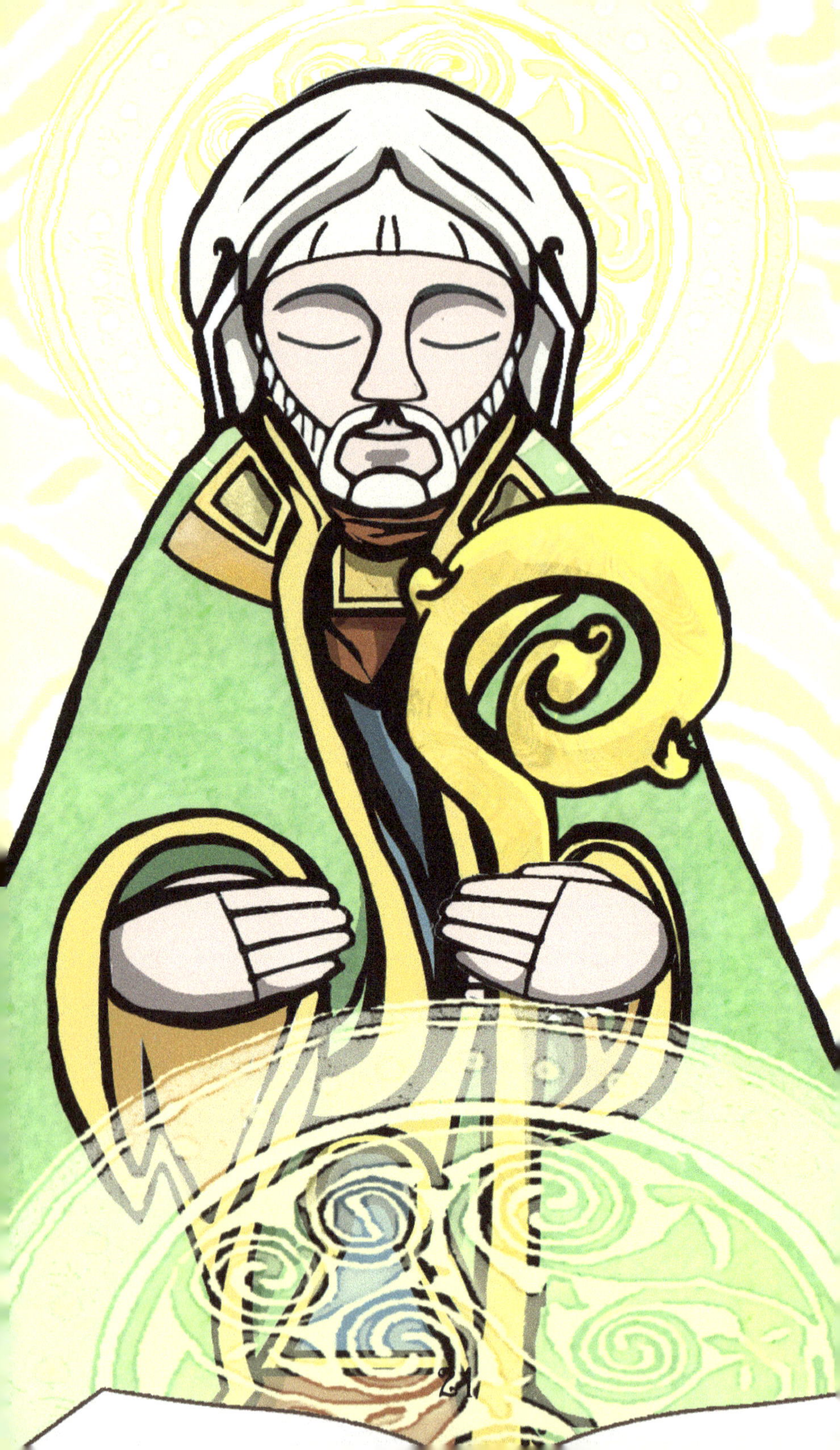

Patrick got to his feet, and
raised his crook.

With the tip of the crook,
he opened the book to
the first page.

And There Was Light

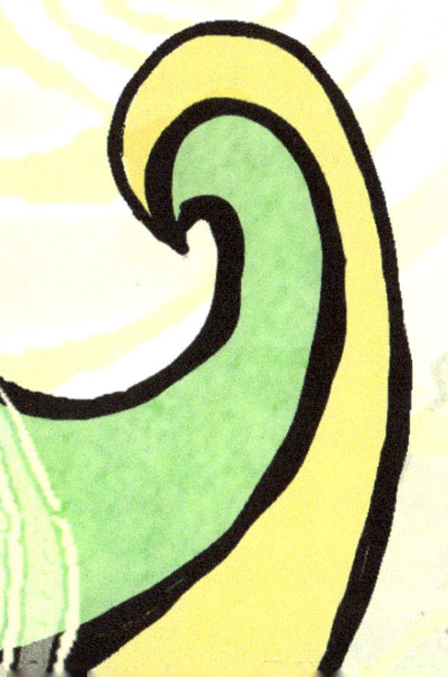

As the men came over
the top of the hill, the
sudden flash confounded
their vision...

When the blindness passed
as it quickly did, they saw
before them Saint Patrick,
seated on the stone, crook
beside him, and a great
book open upon his lap.

Twined in beauty
about the pages was an
illumination of a
   beautiful serpent,
   glinting in the sunlight.
    The men were not
      near enough,
      nor canny enough
        to see the flicker of
        the creature's tongue,
            which to the
              Saint was as
              good as a wink.

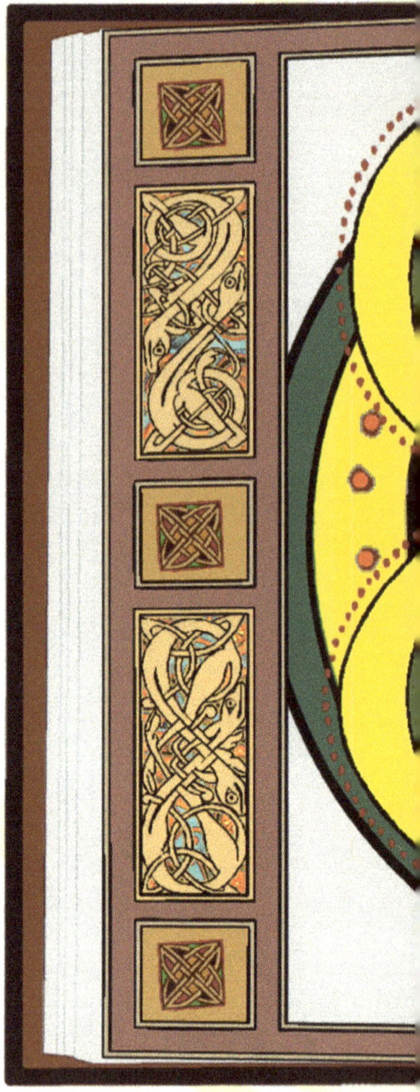

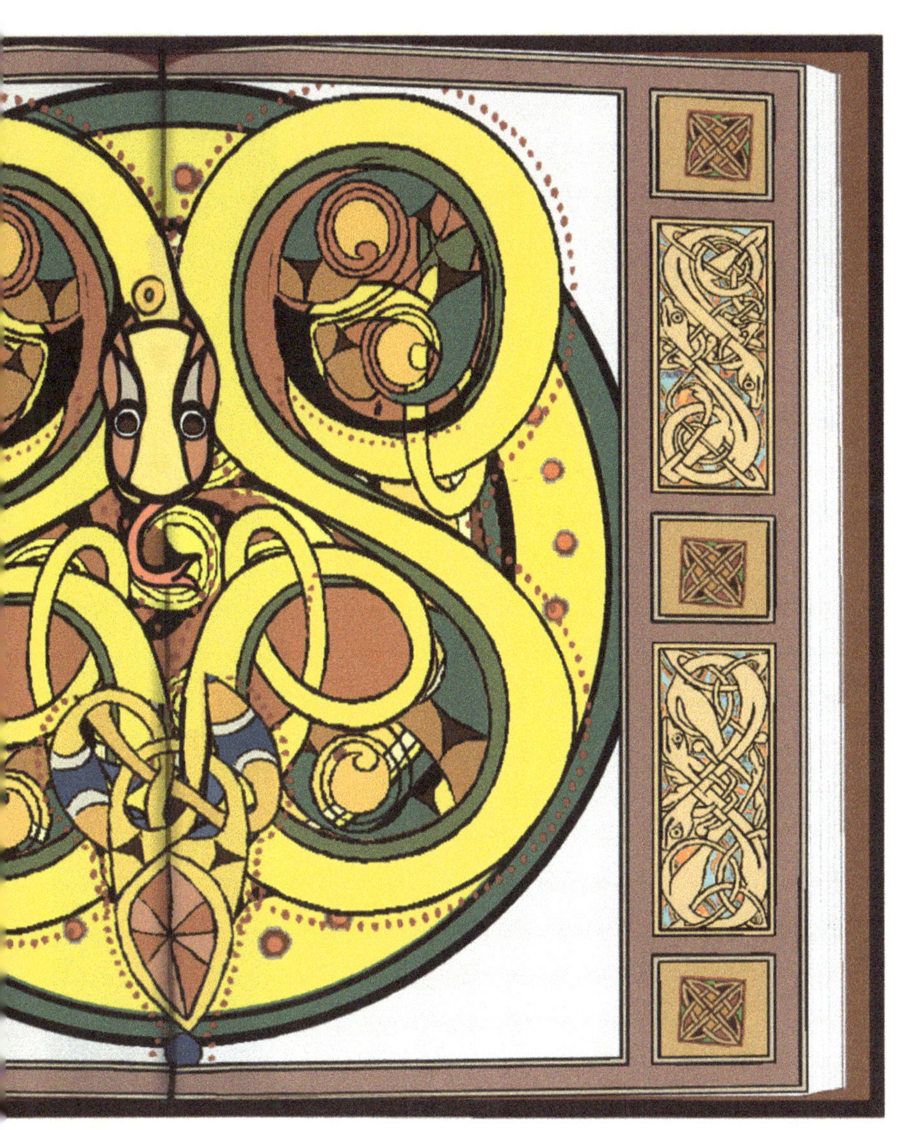

And so the story they still tell,
that Saint Patrick rid the island of Éire of its
serpents, blasting to destruction the very
serpent they pursued, and not knowing mercy
when it happened before their eyes.

24

About the Author

C.L. Redding is a photographer,
writer, and poet of a certain age.
She considers herself an expatriate
of Middle-earth.

About the Artist

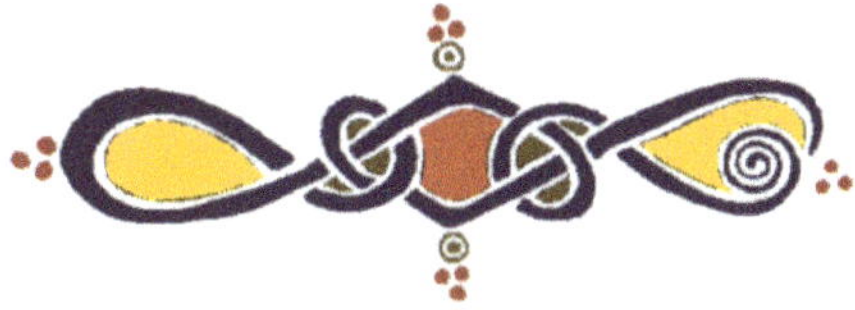

Olivia Wylie is a professional landscaper
who specializes in the restoration of
neglected gardens. When the weather
keeps her indoors, she enjoys researching
and writing about the plants and folklore
she loves, and the ways they've shaped
human thought. She lives in Colorado with a
very patient husband and a rather
impatient cat. Her works can be viewed at
https://www.etsy.com/shop/LeafingOutArt